SALAD DRESSINGS

TERESA H. BURNS

THE CROSSING PRESS SPECIALTY COOKBOOKS

THE CROSSING PRESS · SPECIALTY COOKBOOKS · **FREEDOM, CALIFORNIA**

For information on bulk purchases or group discounts for this and other Crossing Press titles, please contact our Special Sales Manager at 800-777-1048.

The Crossing Press Specialty Cookbook Series

Library of Congress Cataloging-in-Publication Data
Burns, Teresa H.
  Salad Dressings / Teresa H. Burns.
    p. cm. — (The Crossing Press specialty cookbooks series)
  ISBN 0-89594-895-8 (paper)
  1. Salad dressing.   I. Title.   II. Series: Specialty cookbook series
TX819.S27B87 1997
641.8'14—dc21   97-24478
                                                                                    CIP

CONTENTS

INTRODUCTION

Salad is my passion. For the last several years, salad and the consumption of vegetables has been an American fascination as well. There's no reason not to make your own salad dressings. My time-saving secret is to use a hand-held immersion blender that can mix in any sort of wide-mouth jar or glass measuring cup. This handy tool reduces the need for chopping garlic and onions for seasoning, and makes clean-up go particularly fast—a real time-saving device!

The most important thing to remember is that it is easy to have a fresh salad with a fresh dressing every night. You'll soon realize that any and all of my salad dressings go with all types of greens and vegetables in a variety of combinations. Remember, it's always best to use the freshest oils, along with the freshest vegetables, fruits, and herbs. I hope that these recipes inspire you to be creative and to have fun with everyday cooking.

Salad dressings are easy to make; there are no complicated cooking steps to follow. Just look at the recipes and the list of ingredients—they are short and simple. This chapter will give you a few tips for making salad dressings to make the process even easier and more convenient.

Equipment

I have a hand blender—also called an immersion blender—that I use for making most dressings. This small hand-held appliance is a portable blender with enough power to chop ingredients, such as garlic or onion, while blending the liquids. Hand blenders often come with different attachments for blending, whipping, and chopping, but the blending attachment alone works for all salad dressing chores. Also, they often come with their own clear plastic and/or stainless steel mixing containers. These are especially convenient since you can serve directly from the containers, further reducing clean-up time. If your hand blender doesn't have its own container, you can substitute any wide mouth jar or measuring cup and get the same quick and easy results.

Of course, you can use a food processor for making most dressings, but they do present some disadvantages. First, a blender will incorporate more air into a dressing than a food processor; therefore, food processor dressings are a little heavier and have less volume. The other disadvantage is that you will have to transfer the dressing to another container—more dishes to wash.

Most vinaigrettes can be made with a bowl, a whisk, and a little wrist action. Or use a portable hand mixer with just one mixer blade in place in a tall, wide-mouth jar and you have something that works almost as well as hand blender. The mixing blades don't do a good job of chopping, so you will have to chop the herbs, garlic, onion, and other such materials on a cutting board and add to the dressing before or after mixing.

You also need a grater for grating Parmesan cheese, a pepper mill for freshly ground pepper, and a reamer for juicing small quantities of citrus fruits.

Ingredients

Your cupboard should contain an assortment of oils, vinegars, and dried herbs.

Oils. You may think, there's a lot of oil in some of these dressings. That's true, but you only need about 1 tablespoon of dressing per serving, and that turns out to be a very moderate amount of fat.

I like the idea of being able to pick the oil for a recipe. Any oil works. You might choose an extra-virgin oil when you want a rich taste. I like the rich, fruity, almost peppery flavor it gives to a dressing. A few recipes call for walnut oil. Nut oils are delicately flavored and balance the bitter flavor of some greens. Nut oils turn rancid quickly, so it is a good idea to buy them in small bottles and store them in the refrigerator. Peanut oil, sesame oil, and safflower oil are also good. Dark sesame oil, made from toasted seeds, is great with dressings that contain soy sauce. Sesame oil, made from raw sesame seeds, is light in color and flavor.

Vinegars and Citrus Juices. Vinegar or lemon juice or both are used in most dressings to balance the oil. Red and white wine vinegar are made from grapes that were first made into wine. Apple cider vinegar comes from apples and rice vinegar comes from rice. I love the mildly sweet, apple flavor of apple cider vinegar and use it frequently. It is less expensive than the trendy balsamic vinegar and adds a wonderful flavor to a dressing. It's particularly good in coleslaw.

Rice wine vinegar is less acidic than other vinegars. Japanese rice vinegars tend to be sweet, while Chinese rice vinegars are more acidic.

Balsamic vinegar is an Italian red wine vinegar made by boiling the juice of Trebbiano grapes until the sugars caramelize. Then it is aged in oak barrels, like fine wines. The result is a vinegar with a mellow, almost sweet flavor and very dark color. If you aren't paying a premium price for balsamic vinegar, you are getting a cheap imitation made of red wine vinegar flavored with sugar, vanilla, and caramel coloring. Red wine vinegar retains the aroma of the wine from which it is made and is a fairly assertive flavor. White wine vinegar is more delicate and almost neutral in color.

Citrus juices can also be used to add tartness to a dressing. I use fresh lemon juice to bring a fresh, sharp tart flavor to my dressings. Lime juice can also be used, but it is more fruity and less acidic. Orange juice and grapefruit juice can also be used to add a citrusy tartness to a dressing.

There are two types of vinegar I don't use in salad dressings. White vinegar gives a pure, sharp flavor that is fine in pickles but doesn't contribute any flavor to a dressing. I also avoid malt vinegar, which is made from beer, because it has a very strong flavor that doesn't blend well with most dressing ingredients.

Yogurt, buttermilk, vinegar, and lemon juice all will add to the tartness side of the equation. You can balance the tartness with additional oil, or you can use a sweetener.

Mayonnaise and Dairy Products. Sometimes a creamy texture is called for, and that's when mayonnaise, sour cream, yogurt, buttermilk, and/or cheese are used. I use reduced-fat mayonnaise. Those with a sensitive palate will probably notice when their favorite sandwich is made with a reduced-fat mayonnaise, but it generally goes unnoticed in a salad dressing. Of course, you can use regular mayonnaise or fat-free mayonnaise if you prefer.

Sour cream is made from cream that has been cultured with lactic acid. It is rich and adds great body and flavor to a dressing. You can substitute reduced-fat or fat-free sour creams, or yogurt, but taste the dressing. You may have to reduce the quantity of lemon juice or vinegar.

Cottage cheese that has been blended until smooth can be substituted for either yogurt or sour cream. Be sure to taste the dressing and add more vinegar if needed.

Parmesan cheese adds both body and flavor to a dressing. Always use freshly grated Parmesan.

Herbs. When fresh herbs are available, they are a better choice than dried herbs. Unless otherwise stated, I measure fresh herbs by loosely packing the leaves into a measuring cup or spoon. The tough stems are discarded. The chopping can be done with a hand blender after I have measured out the correct amount.

Of all the herbs I use, parsley shows up most frequently, adding a fresh, green flavor to dressings. Both the curly-leaf type and a flat-leaf (Italian) type are available in supermarkets. The latter has a much stronger flavor.

Garlic is another flavor I enjoy in most dressings. If you use a hand blender, you don't even have to bother with mincing or pressing the garlic before combining with the other ingredients.

Anchovies and Worcestershire Sauce. You can't have a proper Caesar salad without anchovies, right? Anchovies or anchovy paste add a briny, pungent flavor to salad dressings. Use either sparingly. Rather than chop the fish, or deal with the leftovers in the can, I prefer anchovy paste in convenient squeeze tubes.

Worcestershire sauce adds a dark, rich, briny, sweet flavor to dressings. It is not as pungent as anchovies, but acts in a similar way to balance the tart ingredients. Worcestershire sauce is made from garlic, soy sauce, tamarind, onions, molasses, lime, anchovies, vinegar, and various spices.

Salt and Pepper. I rarely specify an exact quantity of salt and pepper. Your taste and your dietary requirements should guide you. I do recommend that you don't omit these important flavors all together.

In my pepper grinder, I keep a mix of white, black, and red peppercorns. I use it on everything, including salad dressings. It adds quite a bit of flavor.

Eggs. Several recipes call for eggs, both raw and hard-cooked. In both cases, the eggs are essential for flavor and texture. Raw eggs are added as an emulsifier in many oil-and-vinegar dressings. Vinegar is water-based and won't mix with oil unless you help it along. You can beat the two together to disperse the oil droplets in the vinegar. The second you stop beating, however, the oil and vinegar will separate. Mustard helps to emulsify the mixture, keeping the oil molecules suspended in the vinegar. But an egg yolk works even better. The drawback to raw eggs is the salmonella issue. Farmers and egg producers have been unable to eradicate the salmonella bacteria from their chickens, hence some raw eggs do present a health risk. The danger of salmonella is greatest for the elderly, infants, pregnant women, and people with illnesses or compromised immune systems. Healthy adults should use discretion when it comes to eating raw eggs. Dressings made with raw eggs should be consumed on the day they are made.

Leftover egg whites can be stored for up to four days in a covered glass container in the refrigerator. They can be frozen for up to 1 year. Leftover egg yolks can be covered with water and stored in a covered glass jar for 2 to 3 days. Drain off the water before using.

Hard-cooked eggs present no such health risk. They add a rich flavor and creamy texture to several dressings. Dressings with hard-cooked eggs are particularly well-suited to cooked vegetables, such as asparagus or green beans.

Tips

Cooks who make a lot of soups and stews know that their food often tastes better on the second day. The same holds true for salad dressings. Most of the recipes in this chapter make enough for two or more meals. You can enjoy them on the day they are made, then enjoy them even more on the second day, or you can make them in advance and serve them a day or two later.

Salad dressings should always be stored in an airtight container in the refrigerator. If your dressing has been chilling for more than an hour, it is best to take it out of the refrigerator about 5 minutes before you plan to serve it. Taste the dressing before you put it on the table. You may find that you need to add a little more oil or vinegar because the flavor of the onion or garlic is threatening to overcome the dressing. The flavor of citrus juice sometimes fades and needs to be brightened by an addition of fresh juice. A little more salt often brings the flavors back into balance.

Minor changes in ingredients can make major differences in flavor. Feel free to experiment with different oils, different vinegars, or herbs.

Using Salad Dressings as Marinades

Many oil-and-vinegar dressings can do double-duty as a marinade. In a marinade, the oils help food retain moisture by sealing the surface. The acid (wine, vinegar, or citrus juice) breaks down the tough fibers of the meat and helps to tenderize. The herbs and spices add flavor.

The rule of thumb is to marinate small cuts of meat for about 1 hour before cooking. Marinate large roasts and cuts of meat for several hours or overnight. Firm-fleshed fish and seafood should be marinated for about 30 minutes. Don't overdo the marinating time or you will turn your meat into mush!

Never reuse a marinade that has come in contact with raw meat. Discard it.

BASIC HERB VINAIGRETTE

Any herb will taste delicious in this basic vinaigrette—oregano, basil, thyme, savory, dill—whatever you have on hand. Fresh herbs pack more punch than dried, but dried herbs are okay, too. This versatile vinaigrette can dress any kind of salad—green and leafy, crunchy vegetable, even potato or chicken. It is also a fine marinade for beef, pork, lamb, poultry, or fish.

1/4 cup red wine vinegar
1/2 teaspoon fresh lemon juice
1 tablespoon chopped oregano leaves
    or 3/4 teaspoon dried
1 small garlic clove, minced
3/4 teaspoon dry mustard
1/2 teaspoon sugar
3/4 cup extra-virgin olive oil
Salt and freshly ground pepper

In a small bowl, combine the vinegar, lemon juice, oregano, garlic, mustard, and sugar. Whisk to mix well. Slowly add the oil while whisking, and continue whisking until the mixture is emulsified. Add salt and pepper to taste. Cover and chill the dressing until you are ready to use it. Let stand at room temperature for 5 minutes before whisking again and serving.

You can save time by not chopping the oregano, or mincing the garlic. Simply put everything in a 2 cup or 4 cup glass measuring cup and use a hand blender. This dressing will keep for up to 4 days in an airtight container in the refrigerator.

Yield: About 1 cup

Summertime Herb Vinaigrette

Like the previous recipe, this versatile recipe can dress any type of salad or be used as a marinade for any type of meat or fish. During the summer when fresh herbs are abundant, it is fun to experiment with different combinations of herbs.

2 1/2 tablespoons red wine vinegar
1 tablespoon dry white wine
1 1/2 tablespoons Dijon-style mustard
1 garlic clove, minced
1 tablespoon chopped fresh thyme leaves,
    or 3/4 teaspoon dried
1 tablespoon chopped fresh oregano
    leaves or 3/4 teaspoon dried
1/4 cup vegetable oil
Salt and freshly ground pepper

In a small bowl, combine the vinegar, wine, mustard, garlic, and herbs. Whisk to mix well. Slowly add the oil while whisking, and continue whisking until the mixture is emulsified. Or save time by not mincing the garlic or chopping the herbs. Combine the ingredients in a jar and blend with a hand blender. Add salt and pepper to taste. Check to see if the oil and acid balance is correct. Adjust it if necessary. Cover and chill the dressing until you are ready to use it. Let stand at room temperature for 5 minutes before whisking again and serving.

This dressing will keep for up to 4 days in an airtight container in the refrigerator.

Yield: About 1/2 cup

Mom's Dressing and Marinade

*I learned how to make this dressing from my mother.
It's a very good, basic vinaigrette, with a proportion
of about 1 part vinegar to 2½ parts oil, which is
a fairly rich blend. Fine herbes, a mixture of very
finely chopped herbs, flavors the dressing. The classic
combination for the herb blend is chervil, chives,
parsley, and tarragon, though some commercial mix-
tures combine thyme, sage, oregano, sage, rosemary,
basil, and marjoram. Buy fine herbs in the smallest
quantities you can find and use it within a few
months for best flavor.*

¼ cup red wine vinegar
1 tablespoon fresh lemon juice
2 garlic cloves, minced
2 teaspoon Dijon-style mustard
2 teaspoons sugar
1 teaspoon fine herbes
⅔ cup vegetable oil
Salt and freshly ground pepper

In a small bowl, combine the vinegar, lemon
juice, garlic, mustard, sugar, and herbs. Whisk
to mix well. Slowly add the oil while whisking,
and continue whisking until the mixture is
emulsified. Or combine the ingredients in a jar
and blend with a hand blender. Add salt and
pepper to taste. Cover and chill the dressing
until you are ready to use it. Let stand at room
temperature for 5 minutes before whisking
again and serving.

This dressing will keep for up to 4 days in
an airtight container in the refrigerator.

Yield: About 1 cup

OLIVE AND HERB VINAIGRETTE

Rich black olives, lots of fresh herbs, and sweet red pepper give this vinaigrette extra character. I love this vinaigrette on a green salad! It also makes a distinctive marinade for any meat or fish.

3 tablespoons white wine vinegar
4 teaspoons Dijon-style mustard
1/3 cup extra-virgin olive oil
1/3 cup chopped fresh herbs (basil, chives, tarragon, parsley, mint, etc.)
1/4 cup finely diced red pepper
1/4 cup pitted and chopped Kalamata or other black olives
Salt and freshly ground pepper

In a small bowl, combine the vinegar and mustard. Whisk to mix well. Slowly add the oil while whisking, and continue whisking until the mixture is emulsified. Whisk in the herbs, red pepper, olives, and salt and pepper to taste. Cover and chill the dressing until you are ready to use it. Let stand at room temperature for 5 minutes before whisking again and serving.

This dressing will keep for up to 4 days in an airtight container in the refrigerator.

Yield: About 1 1/4 cups

LEMON AND CAPER VINAIGRETTE

The briny flavor of capers meets the fresh, tart flavor of lemon. This vinaigrette gives salads the sunny flavor of the Mediterranean. As a marinade, it is outstanding with poultry and seafood.

Juice of 1/2 lemon
1 garlic clove, minced
2 tablespoons chopped fresh dill
   or 3/4 teaspoon dried
2 tablespoons chopped fresh parsley
   (preferably Italian)
1/3 cup plus 1 tablespoon vegetable oil
Salt and freshly ground pepper
1 tablespoon capers, rinsed and drained

In a small bowl, combine the lemon juice, garlic, dill, and parsley. Whisk to mix well. Slowly add the oil while whisking, and continue whisking until the mixture is emulsified. Or combine the ingredients in a jar and blend with a hand blender. Add salt and pepper to taste. Stir in the capers. Cover and chill the dressing until you are ready to use it. Let stand at room temperature for 5 minutes before whisking again and serving.

This dressing will keep for up to 4 days in an airtight container in the refrigerator.

Yield: About 1 cup

Mustard and Parsley
Salad Dressing and Marinade

A truly rich blend with a proportion of 4 parts oil to 1 part lemon juice. It is the parsley, however, that carries the day here. This is a lovely dressing for a seafood salad or a marinade for seafood.

3 tablespoons fresh lemon juice
1/2 teaspoon Dijon-style mustard
1 cup chopped fresh parsley (preferably Italian)
1 clove garlic, minced
3/4 cup extra-virgin olive oil
Salt and freshly ground pepper

In a small bowl, combine the lemon juice, mustard, and parsley. Whisk to mix well. Slowly add the oil while whisking, and continue whisking until the mixture is emulsified. Or combine the ingredients in a jar and blend with a hand blender. Add salt and pepper to taste. Cover and chill the dressing until you are ready to use it. Let stand at room temperature for 5 minutes before whisking again and serving.

This dressing will keep for up to 4 days in an airtight container in the refrigerator.

Yield: About 2 cups

PERFECT PESTO VINAIGRETTE

This is wonderful for a pasta salad and a good marinade for poultry or fish. If you have a mortar and pestle or don't mind doing a lot of chopping by hand, you can make this one without a blender, but I think a blender or food processor works best in this case.

1 cup fresh basil leaves
2 tablespoons fresh parsley leaves
   (preferably Italian)
2 garlic cloves
1/4 cup freshly grated Parmesan cheese
2 tablespoons white wine vinegar
2 tablespoons fresh lemon juice
1/2 cup extra-virgin olive oil
Salt and freshly ground pepper

In a jar with a hand blender or in a food processor fitted with a steel blade, combine the basil, parsley, garlic, Parmesan, vinegar, and lemon juice. Blend until the herbs are finely chopped. With the motor running, slowly add the oil and continue processing until the oil is fully incorporated into the mixture. Add salt and pepper to taste. Cover and chill the dressing until you are ready to use it. Let stand at room temperature for 5 minutes before mixing again and serving. Check the dressing to make sure it is balanced acid to oil before using. Adjust if needed.

This dressing will keep for up to 4 days in an airtight container in the refrigerator.

Yield: About 2 cups

Fresh Basil Dijon Vinaigrette

It's always interesting to me how a small change in ingredients can result in a big change in flavor. Here's another basil-based dressing, but the combination of mustard and cider vinegar gives this dressing a tart, spicy flavor.

1/2 cup cider vinegar
1/2 cup fresh basil leaves
1/4 cup fresh parsley (preferably Italian)
2 tablespoons Dijon-style mustard
2 garlic cloves
1 cup vegetable oil
Salt and freshly ground pepper

In a jar with a hand blender or in a food processor fitted with a steel blade, combine the vinegar, basil, parsley, mustard, and garlic. Blend until finely chopped. With the motor running, slowly add the oil and continue processing until the oil is fully incorporated into the mixture. Add salt and pepper to taste. Cover and chill the dressing until you are ready to use it. Let stand at room temperature for 5 minutes before mixing again and serving.

This dressing will keep for up to 4 days in an airtight container in the refrigerator.

Yield: About 2 cups

LEMON SHALLOT
SALAD DRESSING AND MARINADE

Shallots, the underused member of the onion family, come in just the right size for flavoring a small batch of salad dressing. The best thing about a shallot, however, is that it has the taste of both onion and garlic. If you don't have a shallot on hand, you can use either onion or garlic as a substitute.

1 small shallot, peeled
1/4 cup fresh lemon juice
1 to 2 teaspoons sugar, to taste
1/3 cup plus 1 tablespoon vegetable oil
Salt and freshly ground pepper

In a jar with a hand blender or in a food processor fitted with a steel blade, combine the shallot, lemon juice, and 1 teaspoon sugar. Blend until the shallot is finely chopped. With the motor running, slowly add the oil and continue processing until the oil is fully incorporated into the mixture. Add salt and pepper to taste. Taste to see if more sugar is needed. Cover and chill the dressing until you are ready to use it. Let stand at room temperature for 5 minutes before mixing again and serving.

This dressing will keep for up to 4 days in an airtight container in the refrigerator.

Yield: About 3/4 cup

Shallot Vinaigrette

*For using as a marinade for pork and beef,
I particularly like the flavor of dressings made
with cider vinegar, like this one.*

2 tablespoons cider vinegar
1 small shallot
1 small garlic clove
1 teaspoon Dijon-style mustard
1/2 teaspoon Worcestershire sauce
1/2 teaspoon sugar
3/4 cup vegetable oil
Salt and freshly ground pepper

In a jar with a hand blender or in a food processor fitted with a steel blade, combine the vinegar, shallot, garlic, mustard, Worcestershire, and sugar. Blend until the shallot and garlic are finely chopped. With the motor running, slowly add the oil and continue processing until the oil is fully incorporated into the mixture. Add salt and pepper to taste. Cover and chill the dressing until you are ready to use it. Let stand at room temperature for 5 minutes before mixing again and serving.

This dressing will keep for up to 4 days in an airtight container in the refrigerator.

Yield: About 1 cup

RED ONION AND POPPY SEED
SALAD DRESSING AND MARINADE

This sweet-tart dressing is outstanding on a spinach salad. It also makes a fine marinade for beef. The poppy seeds give it a pleasing crunch. Poppy seeds are one of those special-occasion spices that can go stale in the back of the cupboard. Be sure yours taste fresh before using them.

1/3 **cup chopped red onion**
1/4 **cup red wine vinegar**
1 to 2 tablespoons sugar, divided
1/2 **cup vegetable oil**
1/2 **teaspoon poppy seeds**
Salt and white pepper

In a small bowl, combine the onion, vinegar, and 1 tablespoon sugar. Whisk to mix well. Slowly add the oil while whisking, and continue whisking until the mixture is emulsified. Sift in the poppy seeds and add salt and pepper to taste. Check to see if the sugar balance is to your taste and add more if necessary. Cover and chill the dressing until you are ready to use it. Let stand at room temperature for 5 minutes before whisking again and serving.

This dressing will keep for up to 4 days in an airtight container in the refrigerator.

Yield: About 1 1/4 **cups**

CARAMELIZED ONION VINAIGRETTE

The texture of this dressing is rather thick; a little goes a long way. This makes a flavorful marinade for any meat or fish.

3 tablespoons vegetable oil, divided
1/2 onion, thinly sliced
2 to 3 tablespoons balsamic vinegar
1 tablespoon honey
1 teaspoon Dijon-style mustard
Salt and freshly ground pepper

In a small skillet, heat 1 tablespoon of the oil over medium heat. Add the onion and sauté until very soft and golden, about 15 minutes. Let cool.

In a small bowl, combine the onion with the remaining 2 tablespoons oil, 2 tablespoons vinegar, honey, and mustard. Check to see if the balance of oil to vinegar is to your taste. Mix well. Add salt and pepper to taste. Cover and chill the dressing until you are ready to use it. Let stand at room temperature for 5 minutes before mixing again and serving.

This dressing will keep for up to 4 days in an airtight container in the refrigerator.

Yield: About 3/4 cup

BALSAMIC VINAIGRETTE

This Italian-style dressing has both honey and balsamic vinegar to contribute a little extra sweetness, which is nicely balanced by the salty Parmesan and the tart lemon and mustard. The balsamic vinegar gives this dressing a rather dark color, but the flavor is terrific!

2 to 3 tablespoons balsamic vinegar, divided
2 tablespoons honey
1 tablespoon fresh lemon juice
1 tablespoon Dijon-style mustard
1 tablespoon chopped fresh basil or
   1 teaspoon dried
1½ teaspoons freshly grated Parmesan
   cheese
2 garlic cloves, minced
3 tablespoons vegetable oil
Salt and freshly ground pepper

In a small bowl, combine the 2 tablespoons vinegar, honey, lemon juice, mustard, basil, Parmesan, and garlic. Mix well. Slowly add the oil while whisking, and continue whisking until the mixture is emulsified. Check to see if the oil-vinegar-sugar balance is correct and add more vinegar if necessary. Add salt and pepper to taste. Cover and chill the dressing until you are ready to use it. Let stand at room temperature for 5 minutes before whisking again and serving.

This dressing will keep for up to 4 days in an airtight container in the refrigerator.

Yield: About ¾ cup

Warm Balsamic Vinaigrette

When the warm dressing makes contact with sturdy greens, such as spinach, the salad wilts. This texture change is actually quite pleasant; just don't choose this dressing for a baby lettuce or a delicate mesclun mix. It's wonderful on asparagus, grilled leeks, and other cooked vegetables.

1 tablespoon extra-virgin olive oil
3 large shallots, minced
1 garlic clove, minced
2 to 3 tablespoons balsamic vinegar, divided
1 tablespoon Dijon-style mustard
Salt and freshly ground pepper

In a medium-size skillet, heat the oil over medium heat. Add the shallots and garlic and sauté until soft, about 5 minutes. Add 2 tablespoons vinegar, the mustard, and salt and pepper to taste. Mix well. Check the oil-vinegar balance to see if it is to your taste and add more vinegar if necessary. Serve warm.

Yield: About 1/2 cup

APPLE CIDER SALAD DRESSING & MARINADE

A perfect marinade for pork and a delicious dressing for a green salad. Complement the dressing with chopped apples for a lovely fall salad. You'll notice there isn't any salt in the dressing. You can add some, of course, but the flavors are nicely balanced with it.

1 tablespoon apple cider
1 tablespoon cider vinegar
1 tablespoon chopped shallot
2 teaspoons fresh lemon juice
1 teaspoon Dijon-style mustard
1 teaspoon fresh thyme leaves or
**   1/8 teaspoon dried**
1/2 teaspoon Worcestershire sauce
1/4 cup vegetable oil
Freshly ground pepper

In a small bowl, combine the apple cider, vinegar, shallot, lemon juice, mustard, thyme, and Worcestershire. Whisk to mix well. Slowly add the oil while whisking, and continue whisking until the mixture is emulsified. Check to see if the oil-vinegar balance is correct. Add salt and pepper to taste. Check to see if the oil-lemon juice balance is correct. Cover and chill the dressing until you are ready to use it. Let stand at room temperature for 5 minutes before whisking again and serving.

This dressing will keep for up to 7 days in an airtight container in the refrigerator.

Yield: About 1/2 cup

COWBOY VINAIGRETTE

We call this one Cowboy Vinaigrette at my house because it is so robust in flavor—if cowboys ate salad, they'd choose this dressing. The horseradish and cayenne give it a pleasant spicy flavor. I love to crumble a little bacon on top of salads dressed with this vinaigrette. It makes an excellent marinade for beef and pork.

1/3 cup cider vinegar
2 tablespoons chopped onion
1 tablespoon sugar
1 teaspoon Worcestershire sauce
1 teaspoon prepared horseradish
1/2 teaspoon Dijon-style mustard
Pinch cayenne
3/4 cup plus 1 tablespoon vegetable oil
Salt and freshly ground pepper

In a small bowl, combine the vinegar, onion, sugar, Worcestershire, horseradish, mustard, and cayenne. Whisk to mix well. Slowly add the oil while whisking, and continue whisking until the mixture is emulsified. Add salt and pepper to taste. Check the oil-vinegar balance to see if it is correct. Cover and chill the dressing until you are ready to use it. Let stand at room temperature for 5 minutes before whisking again and serving.

This dressing will keep for up to 7 days in an airtight container in the refrigerator.

Yield: About 11/3 cups

MOUNTAIN DRESSING AND VINAIGRETTE

¹/₄ cup finely chopped onion
¹/₄ cup cider vinegar
1 tablespoon finely chopped celery
1 tablespoon finely chopped parsley
1 tablespoon sugar
¹/₄ teaspoon dry mustard
¹/₄ teaspoon paprika
³/₄ cup vegetable oil
Salt and freshly ground pepper

In a small bowl, combine the onion, vinegar, celery, parsley, sugar, dry mustard, and paprika. Whisk to mix well. Slowly add the oil while whisking, and continue whisking until the mixture is emulsified. Add salt and pepper to taste. Cover and chill the dressing until you are ready to use it. Let stand at room temperature for 5 minutes before whisking again and serving.

This dressing will keep for up to 5 days in an airtight container in the refrigerator.

Yield: About 1¹/₂ cups

Humble Honey
Salad Dressing and Marinade

Honey isn't a humble flavor; it is quite distinctive and pairs very nicely with cider vinegar. This dressing is rather sweet. As a marinade, it works best if the marinated meats are to be cooked over indirect heat. Over direct flame, the honey and sugar are liable to result in charring as the sugars caramelize. You'll notice that this recipe calls for celery greens, meaning the leaves at the top of the celery stalk. They add a wonderful fresh flavor to a dressing.

1/3 **cup cider vinegar**
1/4 **to** 1/3 **cup honey, divided**
1 **to 2 tablespoons sugar, divided**
1 **tablespoon finely chopped red onion**
1 **teaspoon Dijon-style mustard**
1/2 **teaspoon finely chopped fresh
    celery greens**
3/4 **cup vegetable oil**
Salt and freshly ground pepper

In a small bowl, combine the vinegar, 1/4 cup honey, 1 tablespoon sugar, onion, mustard, and celery greens. Whisk to mix well. Slowly add the oil while whisking, and continue whisking until the mixture is emulsified. Add salt and pepper to taste. Check to see if there is enough honey and sugar in the dressing. Cover and chill the dressing until you are ready to use it. Let stand at room temperature for 5 minutes before whisking again and serving.

This dressing will keep for up to 7 days in an airtight container in the refrigerator.

Yield: About 13/4 **cups**

Lemon Honey Dressing and Marinade

This is a great marinade for pork. Feel free to add more garlic if you like.

1/3 cup fresh lemon juice
2 to 3 tablespoons honey, divided
1 tablespoon cider vinegar
Dash dry sherry
4 scallions, finely chopped
1 garlic clove, minced
1/2 cup vegetable oil
Salt and freshly ground pepper

In a small bowl, combine the lemon juice, 2 tablespoons honey, vinegar, sherry, scallions, and garlic. Whisk to mix well. Slowly add the oil while whisking, and continue whisking until the mixture is emulsified. Add salt and pepper to taste. Check the oil-lemon juice-honey balance and add more honey if necessary. Cover and chill the dressing until you are ready to use it. Let stand at room temperature for 5 minutes before whisking again and serving.

This dressing will keep for up to 7 days in an airtight container in the refrigerator.

Yield: About 1 cup

CALIFORNIA CITRUS
SALAD DRESSING AND MARINADE

Lemon juice, orange juice, and pink grapefruit juice contribute the tart balance to the oil in this fresh-tasting dressing. It is a great dressing to use on spinach salads, seafood salads, any green salads that include fruit. It is also a wonderful marinade for seafood.

3 tablespoons fresh lemon juice
3 tablespoons fresh pink grapefruit juice
3 tablespoons fresh orange juice
3 tablespoons vegetable oil
1¹/₂ tablespoons finely chopped red onion
2 teaspoons sugar
Salt and freshly ground pepper

In a small bowl or jar, combine all the ingredients. Blend with a hand blender or whisk or shake vigorously. Check the oil-citrus juices balance and adjust if necessary. Cover and chill the dressing until you are ready to use it. Let stand at room temperature for 5 minutes before whisking again and serving.

This dressing will keep for up to 2 days in an airtight container in the refrigerator.

Yield: About ³/₄ cup

Orange Sunshine
Salad Dressing and Marinade

This really does taste like sunshine! Try it as a marinade for duck or any poultry. It can also be served as a dressing for a warm duck salad. You can use any oil in the dressing, but I prefer it with extra-virgin olive oil. The rice wine vinegar is less tart than other vinegars; you can buy it wherever Asian foods are sold.

1/4 cup fresh orange juice
1/4 cup rice wine vinegar
2 tablespoons fresh lemon juice
1 tablespoon sugar
1 teaspoon Dijon-style mustard
1/4 cup oil
Salt and freshly ground pepper

In a small bowl, combine the orange juice, vinegar, lemon juice, sugar, and mustard. Whisk to mix well. Slowly add the oil while whisking, and continue whisking until the mixture is emulsified. Add salt and pepper to taste. Cover and chill the dressing until you are ready to use it. Let stand at room temperature for 5 minutes before whisking again and serving. It's always important to taste the dressing before using it to see if the balance of ingredients is correct.

This dressing will keep for up to 7 days in an airtight container in the refrigerator.

Yield: About 1 cup

Lime Vinaigrette

This is a great fajita marinade. It is also excellent as a marinade for seafood.

3 tablespoons fresh lime juice
2 tablespoons honey
1 tablespoon cider vinegar
1/3 cup vegetable oil
3 tablespoons chopped fresh cilantro
2 tablespoons finely chopped scallions
1/2 teaspoon grated lime zest
Salt and freshly ground pepper

In a small bowl, combine the lime juice, honey, and vinegar. Whisk to mix well. Slowly add the oil while whisking, and continue whisking until the mixture is emulsified. Stir in the cilantro, scallions, and zest. Add salt and pepper to taste. Cover and chill the dressing until you are ready to use it. Let stand at room temperature for 5 minutes before whisking again and serving.

This dressing will keep for up to 2 days in an airtight container in the refrigerator.

Yield: About 1 cup

GREAT GRAPEFRUIT-HONEY
SALAD DRESSING AND MARINADE

3 tablespoons cider vinegar
3 tablespoons fresh grapefruit juice
2 tablespoons honey
1 garlic clove, minced
Pinch cayenne
¼ cup vegetable oil
Salt and freshly ground pepper

In a small bowl, combine the vinegar, grapefruit juice, honey, garlic, and cayenne. Whisk to mix well. Slowly add the oil while whisking, and continue whisking until the mixture is emulsified. Add salt and pepper to taste. Cover and chill the dressing until you are ready to use it. Let stand at room temperature for 5 minutes before whisking again and serving.

This dressing will keep for up to 4 days in an airtight container in the refrigerator.

Yield: About ¾ cup

Nutty Maple
Salad Dressing and Marinade

The combination of walnut oil, maple syrup, and cider vinegar makes a dressing of surprising subtlety that is wonderful on a green salad. It also makes an excellent all-purpose marinade.

2 tablespoons cider vinegar
2 tablespoons fresh lemon juice
2 tablespoons finely chopped shallots
1 tablespoon pure maple syrup
1 teaspoon sugar
1/2 teaspoon dry mustard
1/3 cup walnut oil
Salt and freshly ground pepper

In a small bowl, combine the vinegar, lemon juice, shallots, maple syrup, sugar, and mustard. Whisk to mix well. Slowly add the oil while whisking, and continue whisking until the mixture is emulsified. Add salt and pepper to taste. Cover and chill the dressing until you are ready to use it. Let stand at room temperature for 5 minutes before whisking again and serving.

This dressing will keep for up to 7 days in an airtight container in the refrigerator.

Yield: About 3/4 cup

Hazelnut Vinaigrette

Hazelnuts have become popular in recent years as a flavoring for deserts and confections, even for coffee. They also make a rich, aromatic contribution to a salad.

1/4 cup raw hazelnuts
3 tablespoons white wine vinegar
1 teaspoon Dijon-style mustard
3 tablespoons hazelnut or walnut oil
3 tablespoons extra-virgin olive oil
1 scallion, finely chopped
Salt and freshly ground pepper

First, toast the hazelnuts. Preheat the oven to 350° F. Place the nuts in a single layer in a baking pan and bake for 10 to 15 minutes, or until they are lightly colored, and the skins are beginning to blister. Remove from the oven. Wrap the nuts in a clean kitchen towel and allow them to steam for 1 minute. Rub the nuts with the towel to remove the skins and let them cool. Then chop them in a food processor. Remove them from the food processor and set aside.

In the same bowl of the food processor, combine the vinegar and mustard and process to mix. With the motor running, slowly add the oils and continue processing until the mixture is emulsified. Pour into a small bowl or jar and stir in the nuts and scallion. Add salt and pepper to taste. Cover and chill the dressing until you are ready to use it. Let stand at room temperature for 5 minutes before mixing again and serving.

This dressing will keep for up to 6 days in an airtight container in the refrigerator.

Yield: About 3/4 cup

Spicy Green Chile Dressing and Marinade

This wonderful dressing has only 12 calories per serving. It is light on oil, but rich with flavor! It makes an excellent barbecue sauce for meat and chicken.

1 (4-ounce) can green chiles, diced
1/2 cup cider vinegar
5 tablespoons ketchup
1 tablespoon vegetable oil
1 tablespoon chopped fresh parsley
   (preferably Italian)
2 garlic cloves
1 teaspoon sugar
Salt and freshly ground pepper

In a jar with a hand blender or in a food processor or blender, combine all the ingredients, adding salt and pepper to taste. Process to mix. Cover and chill the dressing until you are ready to use it. Let stand at room temperature for 5 minutes before mixing again and serving. Check to see that the dressing is balanced to your taste. You can add more sugar (a bit) or more vinegar if you like.

This dressing will keep for up to 2 weeks in an airtight container in the refrigerator.

Yield: About 1 cup

Tomato Vinaigrette

2 medium-size tomatoes, peeled, seeded,
   and quartered*
3 tablespoons balsamic vinegar
3 tablespoons cider vinegar
1 garlic clove
1/4 teaspoon ground cumin
Pinch cayenne
1 cup plus 1 tablespoon extra-virgin
   olive oil
3 tablespoons chopped fresh cilantro
Salt

In a jar with a hand blender or in a food processor, combine the tomatoes, vinegars, garlic, cumin, and cayenne. Briefly process to mix, but do not completely purée the tomatoes. With the motor running, slowly add the oil until the mixture is emulsified. Stir in the cilantro and salt to taste. Cover and chill the dressing until you are ready to use it. Let stand at room temperature for 5 minutes before mixing again and serving.

This dressing will keep for up to 6 days in an airtight container in the refrigerator.

*Note: The best way to remove the skin from tomatoes is to dip the tomatoes in boiling water for 30 seconds. Then quickly run cold water over them to stop the cooking process. The skins should just slip off. To seed a tomato, cut in half and gently squeeze out the seeds.

Yield: About 2 cups

TANGY TOMATO DRESSING AND MARINADE

A chopped jalapeño enlivens this dressing. This is a great dressing to use with a taco salad or any salad served with a Mexican dish. It makes a delicious marinade for any meat.

1/2 **cup fresh cilantro leaves**
2 **garlic cloves**
1 **jalapeño, peeled and seeded (optional)***
1 **cup peeled, seeded, and chopped tomato**
   (see page 39)
3 **tablespoons red wine vinegar**
2 **tablespoons fresh lemon juice**
1 **teaspoon ground cumin**
1/2 **teaspoon dried oregano**
10 **tablespoons vegetable oil**
Salt and freshly ground pepper

In a jar with a hand blender or in a bowl of a food processor fitted with a steel blade, combine the cilantro, garlic, and jalapeño. Process briefly until chopped. Add the tomato, vinegar, lemon juice, cumin, and oregano and process to blend well. Slowly add the oil, processing until the mixture is emulsified. Add salt and pepper to taste. Cover and chill the dressing until you are ready to use it. Let stand at room temperature for 5 minutes before mixing again and serving.

This dressing will keep for up to 4 days in an airtight container in the refrigerator.

*Note: To peel a jalapeño or other chile, cut the chile in half and seed. Rub oil on the skin. Place on a baking sheet, skin side up, and broil for 1 to 3 minutes. Place the chile in a plastic bag to steam for 5 minutes. The skin should just slip off. Make sure you wash your hands after handling the hot chiles.

Yield: About 1 1/2 cups

CATALINA SALAD DRESSING

The origins of this salad dressing are obscure, but its popularity is unquestioned. This is a family favorite. It makes an excellent, all-purpose marinade.

1/3 cup ketchup
1/4 to 1/3 cup sugar, divided
1/4 cup white wine vinegar
1 small onion, chopped
3/4 cup vegetable oil
Salt and freshly ground pepper

In the bowl of a food processor fitted with a steel blade or in a bowl with a hand blender, combine the ketchup, 1/4 cup sugar, vinegar, and onion. Process until the onion is finely chopped. Slowly add the oil, processing until the mixture is emulsified. Add salt and pepper to taste. Taste to see if the amount of sugar is correct. Add some if necessary. Cover and chill the dressing until you are ready to use it. Let stand at room temperature for 5 minutes before mixing again and serving.

This dressing will keep for up to 2 weeks in an airtight container in the refrigerator.

Yield: About 3/4 cup

AMERICAN "FRENCH" DRESSING AND MARINADE

Kids love this American classic! It is quite similar to Catalina Salad Dressing, but the change from wine vinegar to cider vinegar and the addition of Worcestershire sauce makes a fairly significant difference in flavor.

1 cup vegetable oil
1/4 to 1/2 cup sugar, divided
1/3 cup ketchup
1/4 cup cider vinegar
3 tablespoons finely chopped onion
2 teaspoons Worcestershire sauce
Salt and freshly ground pepper

In a jar with a hand blender or in a food processor fitted with a steel blade, combine all the ingredients. Use only 1/4 cup sugar. Blend until well mixed. Check the balance of oil-vinegar-sugar. If you like more sugar, add the remaining sugar and blend. Cover and chill the dressing until you are ready to use it. Let stand at room temperature for 5 minutes before mixing again and serving.

This dressing will keep for up to 2 weeks in an airtight container in the refrigerator.

Yield: About 2 cups

Bloody Mary
Salad Dressing and Marinade

Tomato juice acts as a fat-free moisture extender in this dressing. Notice that there is only 2½ tablespoons of oil used in this recipe.

⅓ cup canned tomato juice
¼ cup cider vinegar
2½ tablespoons vegetable oil
2 tablespoons chopped fresh basil or
  ¾ teaspoon dried
1 teaspoon fresh lemon or lime juice
2 teaspoons sugar
1 teaspoon Dijon-style mustard
1 garlic clove, minced
Dash Tabasco sauce
Dash Worcestershire sauce
Salt and freshly ground pepper

In a jar with a hand blender or in a food processor fitted with a steel blade, combine all the ingredients, adding salt and pepper to taste. Blend until well mixed. Cover and chill the dressing until you are ready to use it. Let stand at room temperature for 5 minutes before mixing again and serving.

This dressing will keep for up to 2 weeks in an airtight container in the refrigerator.

Yield: About 1 cup

SUNNY DRIED TOMATO VINAIGRETTE

1/4 **cup chopped sun-dried tomatoes**
1/4 **cup chopped roasted red pepper**
2 **tablespoons white wine vinegar**
2 **tablespoons balsamic vinegar**
2 **tablespoons chopped fresh parsley**
   (preferably Italian)
1 **garlic clove**
1/3 **cup vegetable oil**

In a jar with a hand blender or in a food processor fitted with a steel blade, combine the tomatoes, pepper, vinegars, parsley, and garlic. Process until the garlic and tomatoes are very finely chopped. Slowly add the oil, processing until the mixture is emulsified. Add salt and pepper to taste. Cover and chill the dressing until you are ready to use it. Let stand at room temperature for 5 minutes before mixing again and serving.

This dressing will keep for up to 1 week in an airtight container in the refrigerator.

Yield: About 1 cup

Tomato Tarragon
Salad Dressing and Marinade

Tarragon's distinctive aniselike flavor blends well with tomato. This dressing is delicious with assertive greens. It makes an excellent all-purpose marinade.

2 small tomatoes, peeled and seeded (see page 39)
1 shallot
2 tablespoons white wine vinegar
1 tablespoon Dijon-style mustard
2 teaspoons fresh tarragon or
  1/2 teaspoon dried
1/4 cup vegetable oil
Salt and freshly ground pepper

In a jar with a hand blender or in a food processor, combine the tomatoes, shallot, vinegar, mustard, and tarragon. Process until the shallot is finely chopped. Slowly add the oil, processing until the mixture is emulsified. Add salt and pepper to taste. Cover and chill the dressing until you are ready to use it. Let stand at room temperature for 5 minutes before mixing again and serving.

This dressing will keep for up to 4 days in an airtight container in the refrigerator.

Yield: About 1 1/4 cups

Salsa Vinaigrette

This recipe also doubles as a salsa, to use with chips or any Tex-Mex dish. If the thought of jalapeño heats you up, roast if first for a milder flavor. Remember always to wash your hands and any utensils thoroughly after handling hot peppers.

1 cup peeled, seeded, and chopped
  tomatoes (see page 39)
1/2 cup loosely packed cilantro leaves,
  chopped
1/3 cup plus 2 tablespoons vegetable oil
3 tablespoons fresh lemon juice
3 tablespoons red wine vinegar
3 scallions, finely chopped
2 garlic cloves, minced
1 jalapeño, seeded and minced
1 tablespoon fresh oregano or
  1/2 teaspoon dried
1/2 teaspoon ground cumin

Combine all the ingredients in a jar or bowl and shake or stir. Cover and refrigerate the dressing until you are ready to use it. Let stand at room temperature for 5 minutes before mixing again and serving.

This dressing will keep for up to 2 days in an airtight container in the refrigerator.

Yield: About 2 1/2 cups

CURRY VINAIGRETTE

*This is an excellent marinade for chicken
and seafood.*

1/2 cup white wine vinegar
1 garlic clove
2 tablespoons light brown sugar
2 tablespoons chopped fresh chives
1 teaspoon curry powder
1 teaspoon soy sauce
1/2 cup vegetable oil

In a jar with a hand blender or in a food processor fitted with a steel blade, combine the vinegar, garlic, sugar, chives, curry, and soy sauce. Blend until the garlic is finely chopped. Slowly add the oil, processing until the mixture is emulsified. Cover and chill the dressing until you are ready to use it. Let stand at room temperature for 5 minutes before mixing again and serving.

This dressing will keep for up to 1 week in an airtight container in the refrigerator.

Yield: About 1¹/₄ cups

WASABI VINAIGRETTE

Wasabi is a hot Japanese condiment that is traditionally used in sushi. You may have to adjust the amount you use as different brands have different levels of heat.

2 tablespoons cider vinegar
1 tablespoon fresh lemon juice
1 tablespoon wasabi
2 garlic cloves
1 teaspoon sugar
1/4 cup vegetable oil
2 tablespoons chopped fresh cilantro
1 teaspoon fresh thyme or
    1/2 teaspoon dried
Salt and freshly ground pepper

In a jar with a hand blender or in a bowl of a food processor fitted with a steel blade, combine the vinegar, lemon juice, wasabi, garlic, and sugar. Blend until the garlic is finely chopped. Slowly add the oil, processing until the mixture is emulsified. Stir in the cilantro, thyme, and salt and pepper to taste. Cover and chill the dressing until you are ready to use it. Let stand at room temperature for 5 minutes before mixing again and serving.

This dressing will keep for up to 4 days in an airtight container in the refrigerator.

Yield: About 3/4 cup

Thai Dressing and Marinade

This dressing gets quite a bit of fire from red pepper flakes—use less if you don't like hot foods. This makes an excellent marinade for poultry and seafood.

6 tablespoons fresh lime juice
¼ cup vegetable oil
¼ cup soy sauce
3 garlic cloves, minced
1¼ tablespoons peanut butter
1 tablespoon red pepper flakes
Salt and freshly ground pepper

Combine all the ingredients in a bowl or jar and stir or shake to blend well.

Cover and chill the dressing until you are ready to use it. Let stand at room temperature for 5 minutes before stirring or shaking again and serving.

This dressing will keep for up to 1 week in an airtight container in the refrigerator.

Yield: About 1 cup

CHUTNEY SALAD DRESSING AND MARINADE

This makes a very interesting dressing for a green salad or rice-based salad. Or use it as a marinade for poultry. Sesame oil and chutney give the dressing an Asian identity.

1/2 cup toasted sesame oil
1/2 cup fruit chutney (such as mango, cherry, or apricot)
1/4 cup cider vinegar
2 garlic cloves, minced
1 tablespoon soy sauce
1 tablespoon Dijon-style mustard
Dash Tabasco sauce

Combine all the ingredients in a bowl or jar and stir or shake to blend well.

Cover and chill the dressing until you are ready to use it. Let stand at room temperature for 5 minutes before stirring or shaking again and serving.

This dressing will keep for up to 2 weeks in an airtight container in the refrigerator.

Yield: About 1 1/2 cups

Asian Salad Dressing and Marinade

In this dressing, it is the combination of sesame oil, garlic, ginger, soy sauce, and mirin that creates the characteristic Asian flavor. Mirin is a sweet rice wine. It is found in Japanese markets and many grocery stores.

1/4 cup rice wine vinegar
3 tablespoons vegetable oil
2 tablespoons toasted sesame oil
2 tablespoons soy sauce
2 tablespoons sugar
1 tablespoon mirin
1 tablespoon fresh lemon juice
2 garlic cloves, minced
1 teaspoon minced ginger
1/8 teaspoon Tabasco sauce

Combine all the ingredients in a bowl or jar and stir or shake to blend well.

Cover and chill the dressing until you are ready to use it. Let stand at room temperature for 5 minutes before stirring or shaking again and serving.

This dressing will keep for up to 2 weeks in an airtight container in the refrigerator.

Yield: About 1 cup

Seedy Cilantro
Salad Dressing and Marinade

Cilantro is an herb that you either love or hate. It has a distinctive musky flavor. It is used extensively in the cooking of Mexico and Southeast Asia. This dressing is Asian in character.

¹/4 **cup toasted sesame seeds***
3 **tablespoons rice vinegar**
2¹/2 **tablespoons fresh lemon juice**
1 **tablespoon sake or sherry**
1 **tablespoon soy sauce**
1 **garlic cloves**
1 **cup fresh cilantro leaves**
2 **tablespoons toasted sesame oil**
¹/3 **cup peanut oil**
Salt and freshly ground pepper

In a jar with a hand blender or in a bowl of a food processor fitted with a steel blade, combine the sesame seeds, vinegar, lemon juice, sake, soy sauce, and garlic. Process until the garlic is finely chopped. Add the cilantro and sesame oil and blend again. Slowly add the peanut oil, processing until the mixture is emulsified. Stir in the salt and pepper to taste. Cover and chill the dressing until you are ready to use it. Let stand at room temperature for 5 minutes before mixing again and serving.

This dressing will keep for up to 2 days in an airtight container in the refrigerator.

*Note: To toast sesame seeds, place the seeds in a dry skillet over medium heat and cook, stirring constantly for about 3 minutes, until golden and fragrant.

Yield: About 1¹/3 cups

TAHINI DRESSING AND MARINADE

If you haven't yet enjoyed the flavor of tahini in a Middle Eastern dish, this dressing is a good way to begin. Tahini is a paste made of raw sesame seeds, similar in consistency to peanut butter.

1/3 cup vegetable oil
3 tablespoons fresh lemon juice
2 tablespoons tahini
1 garlic clove, minced
Dash Tabasco sauce
Salt and freshly ground pepper

Combine all the ingredients in a bowl or jar and stir to blend well.

Cover and chill the dressing until you are ready to use it. Serve at room temperature.

This dressing will keep for up to 2 weeks in an airtight container in the refrigerator.

Yield: About 2/3 cup

Spinach Salad Dressing 1

1 tablespoon warm bacon drippings
1 small onion, minced
2 tablespoons dry sherry
2 tablespoons honey
4 bacon slices, fried and crumbled
Freshly ground pepper

Combine the bacon drippings, onion, sherry, and honey in a bowl or jar and stir or shake to blend well.

Toss with the spinach and top the salad with the bacon and pepper. Serve at once.

Yield: About 1/3 cup

Spinach Salad Dressing 2

5 slices bacon, fried and crumbled
2/3 cup bacon drippings
5 tablespoons cider vinegar
2 tablespoons fresh lemon juice
1 tablespoon sugar
3/4 teaspoons Worcestershire sauce
Freshly ground pepper
2 tablespoons brandy

Combine the bacon, bacon drippings, vinegar, lemon juice, sugar, Worcestershire, and pepper in a skillet. Heat until hot. Add the brandy and ignite.

Pour over the salad and serve immediately.

Yield: About 1 1/2 cups

REAL ROQUEFORT DRESSING

Roquefort is one of the oldest and best loved cheeses in the world. A creamy blue cheese made from sheep's milk, it has been enjoyed since Roman times and was said to be a favorite of Charlemagne. The name "Roquefort" is protected by law to mean only blue cheese that is aged in the caverns of Mount Combalou near the village of Roquefort. If you want the real stuff, be sure the package has a red sheep on the wrapper.

1/4 cup rice wine vinegar
2 tablespoons fresh thyme leaves or
   3/4 teaspoon dried
1 teaspoon Dijon-style mustard
1 garlic clove
1/2 cup extra-virgin olive oil
1/4 cup crumbled Roquefort cheese
Salt and freshly ground pepper

In a jar with a hand blender or in a food processor fitted with a steel blade, combine the vinegar, thyme, mustard, and garlic. Blend until the garlic is finely chopped. Slowly add the oil, processing until the mixture is emulsified. Stir in the cheese and salt and pepper to taste. Cover and chill the dressing until you are ready to use it. Let stand at room temperature for 5 minutes before mixing again and serving.

This dressing will keep for up to 5 days in an airtight container in the refrigerator.

Yield: About 1 cup

Italian Parmesan Salad Dressing

Most cheese dressings are creamy in consistency. I like the combination of oil, vinegar, and cheese.

1/3 cup balsamic vinegar
1/4 cup freshly grated Parmesan cheese
1 1/2 tablespoons fresh lemon juice
2 scallions, chopped
2 teaspoons Worcestershire sauce
2 garlic cloves
1 tablespoon fresh oregano leaves or
   1 teaspoon dried
1/2 cup plus 1 tablespoon vegetable oil
Dash Tabasco sauce
Salt and freshly ground pepper

In a jar with a hand blender or in a food processor fitted with a steel blade, combine the vinegar, Parmesan, lemon juice, scallions, Worcestershire, garlic, and oregano. Blend until the garlic and oregano are finely chopped. Slowly add the oil, processing until the mixture is emulsified. Stir in the Tabasco and salt and pepper to taste. Cover and chill the dressing until you are ready to use it. Let stand at room temperature for 5 minutes before mixing again and serving.

This dressing will keep for up to 7 days in an airtight container in the refrigerator.

Variation: Replace the oregano with 3/4 teaspoon *fine herbes*.

Yield: About 1 1/2 cups

CAESAR SALAD DRESSING
WITH BLUE CHEESE 4

Caesar Salad is traditionally made with Parmesan cheese, but blue cheese can give it extra punch.

1/4 cup extra-virgin olive oil
1 garlic clove
2 tablespoons anchovy paste
4 tablespoons crumbled blue cheese, divided
2 1/2 tablespoons fresh lemon juice
1/2 teaspoon Worcestershire sauce
1 egg
1/4 cup Parmesan cheese
Salt and freshly ground pepper

In a jar with a hand blender or in a food processor fitted with a steel blade, combine the oil, garlic, anchovy paste, and 2 tablespoons of the blue cheese. Blend until the garlic is finely chopped. Add the lemon juice, Worcestershire, egg, and Parmesan cheese and stir or shake well.

Dress the salad and sprinkle the top with the remaining blue cheese. Serve at once.

Yield: About 3/4 cup

LIGHT AND ZESTY
CAESAR SALAD DRESSING 5

Not everyone likes anchovies, so this version gets its punch from mustard instead. This one also omits the egg, which makes it possible to store the leftover dressing and/or make the dressing in advance.

2 tablespoons Dijon-style mustard
1 tablespoon lemon juice
1 teaspoon Worcestershire sauce
2 teaspoons sugar
$1/2$ cup vegetable oil
$1^1/2$ tablespoons freshly grated
   Parmesan cheese
Salt and freshly ground pepper

In a jar with a hand blender or in a food processor fitted with a steel blade, combine the mustard, lemon juice, Worcestershire, and sugar. Blend to mix. Slowly add the oil, processing until the mixture is emulsified. Stir in the Parmesan cheese and salt and pepper to taste. Cover and chill the dressing until you are ready to use it. Let stand at room temperature for 5 minutes before mixing again and serving.

This dressing will keep for up to 2 weeks in an airtight jar in the refrigerator.

Yield: About $3/4$ cup

GORGONZOLA SALAD DRESSING

Gorgonzola from Italy is one of the world's great cheeses. Made from cow's milk, it is rich, creamy, and fairly pungent. A little goes a long way in flavoring a dressing.

1/2 cup crumbled Gorgonzola cheese
1/3 cup vegetable oil
2 tablespoons fresh lemon juice
2 tablespoons white wine vinegar
2 tablespoons sour cream
1 teaspoon Dijon-style mustard
1 teaspoon sugar
1 garlic clove, minced
Salt and freshly ground pepper

In a jar with a hand blender or in a food processor fitted with a steel blade, combine all the ingredients, adding salt pepper to taste. Blend until well-mixed. Cover and chill the dressing until you are ready to use it. Let stand at room temperature for 5 minutes before serving.

This dressing will keep for up to 4 days in an airtight container in the refrigerator.

Variation: Instead of the Gorgonzola, experiment with Roquefort, feta, or Romano cheese.

Yield: About 1 1/4 cups

Bold Balsamic Salad Dressing

2 tablespoons balsamic vinegar
2 tablespoons oil
2 tablespoons yogurt
1 teaspoon fresh lemon juice
1 teaspoon Dijon-style mustard
1 shallot, minced
Salt and freshly ground pepper

Combine all the ingredients in a bowl or jar. Stir or shake to combine well. Check the oil-acid balance. Cover and chill the dressing until you are ready to use it. Let stand at room temperature for 5 minutes before mixing again and serving.

This dressing will keep for up to 5 days in an airtight container in the refrigerator.

Yield: About $1/2$ cup

Sweet and Sour Salad Dressing

This is a good dressing for coleslaw.

2 egg yolks
1/4 cup sugar
3 tablespoons red wine vinegar
Juice of 1/2 lemon
1 teaspoon dry mustard
1/2 teaspoon white pepper
1/2 cup vegetable oil
Salt

In a jar with a hand blender or in a food processor fitted with a steel blade, combine the eggs, sugar, vinegar, lemon juice, mustard, and pepper. Blend until well mixed. Slowly add the oil, processing until the mixture is emulsified. Stir in salt to taste. Serve at once.

Yield: About 1 1/2 cups

OLD WORLD DRESSING

1/4 cup red wine vinegar
2 tablespoons cream
1 1/2 teaspoons Dijon-style mustard
1 1/2 teaspoons Worcestershire sauce
1 teaspoon egg yolk
1 teaspoon A-1 steak sauce
2 garlic cloves
2/3 cup vegetable oil
Salt and freshly ground pepper

In a jar with a hand blender or in a food processor fitted with a steel blade, combine the vinegar, cream, mustard, Worcestershire, egg, steak sauce, and garlic. Blend until the garlic is finely chopped. Slowly add the oil, processing until the mixture is emulsified. Stir in the salt and pepper to taste. Serve at once.

Yield: About 1 cup

DILLY SALAD DRESSING

A delicious dressing for potato salad.

1 egg yolk
¹/₂ cup white wine vinegar
1 small onion, chopped
1¹/₂ teaspoons Dijon-style mustard
1 cup vegetable oil
1 teaspoon mayonnaise (reduced-fat
   is acceptable)
1¹/₂ tablespoons fresh dill
Salt and freshly ground pepper

In the bowl of a food processor fitted with a steel blade or in a bowl with a hand blender, combine the egg, vinegar, onion, and mustard. Process until the onion is finely chopped. Slowly add the oil, processing until the mixture is emulsified. Stir in the mayonnaise, dill, and salt and pepper to taste. Serve at once.

Yield: About 1¹/₂ cups

German Salad Dressing

I like to make this dressing quite peppery.

Juice of 1/2 lemon
3 tablespoons extra-virgin olive oil
2 garlic cloves
1 to 2 tablespoons honey, divided
1/2 teaspoon dry mustard
2 1/2 tablespoons whipping cream
Salt and freshly ground pepper

In a jar with a hand blender or in a food processor fitted with a steel blade, combine the lemon juice, oil, garlic, 1 tablespoon honey, and mustard. Blend until the garlic is finely chopped. Stir in the cream and salt and pepper to taste. Cover and chill the dressing until you are ready to use it. Let stand at room temperature for 5 minutes before mixing again and serving. Taste to see if the balance of sweet and sour is to your taste. If not, add the remaining honey.

This will keep for up to 2 days in an airtight container in the refrigerator.

Yield: About 3/4 cup

TEMPTING TARRAGON SALAD DRESSING

2 tablespoons rice wine vinegar
1 tablespoon Dijon-style mustard
1½ tablespoons fresh tarragon or
    1 teaspoon dried
½ teaspoon sugar
⅓ cup extra-virgin olive oil
1 tablespoon mayonnaise (reduced-fat
    is acceptable)
Salt and freshly ground pepper

In a jar with a hand blender or in a food processor fitted with a steel blade, combine the vinegar, mustard, tarragon, and sugar. Process until the tarragon is finely chopped. Slowly add the oil, processing until the mixture is emulsified. Stir in the mayonnaise and salt and pepper to taste. Cover and chill the dressing until you are ready to use it. Let stand at room temperature for 5 minutes before mixing again and serving.

This will keep for up to 5 days in an airtight container in the refrigerator.

Yield: About ⅔ cup

MEAN GREEN SALAD DRESSING

If you like, you can add a few drops of green food coloring for a deeper color.

1 egg yolk
2 tablespoons white wine vinegar
2 tablespoons chopped fresh chives
2 tablespoons chopped fresh parsley
   (preferably Italian)
1 tablespoon chopped onion
1 garlic clove
1 teaspoon anchovy paste
3/4 cup vegetable oil
1/4 cup whipping cream
Salt and freshly ground pepper

In a jar with a hand blender or in a food processor fitted with a steel blade, combine the egg, vinegar, chives, parsley, onion, garlic, and anchovy paste. Process until the garlic and herbs are finely chopped. Slowly add the oil, processing until the mixture is emulsified. Stir in the cream and salt and pepper to taste. Serve at once.

Yield: About 1 1/2 cups

HOMEMADE MAYONNAISE, USING A WHISK

The flavor of homemade mayonnaise is so superior to the store-bought kind that you may find yourself making this again and again. You may have heard that mayonnaise is tricky to make. It isn't really, but you have to add the oil slowly so that the yolks can blend together with no difficulty. Eggs can hold only so much oil, so it is important not to exceed the limit.

2 egg yolks, at room temperature
1 teaspoon white wine vinegar
1 teaspoon Dijon-style mustard
1¹/₂ cups vegetable oil
Lemon juice, to taste
Salt and freshly ground pepper

Combine egg yolks, 1 teaspoon vinegar, mustard, salt, and pepper. Blend with a hand blender. Add ¹/₂ cup of the oil SLOWLY while blending. Add the rest of the vinegar. Then add the remaining oil in a stream, blending constantly. Blend in lemon juice and serve. Cover and chill until ready to use.

The trick here is to add the oil slowly so that the yolks can blend together with no difficulty. Egg can only hold so much oil, so it is important not to exceed the limit.

Yield: About 2 cups

HOMEMADE MAYONNAISE, USING A BLENDER

2 egg yolks, at room temperature
2 teaspoons white wine vinegar, divided
1 teaspoon Dijon-style mustard
1½ cups vegetable oil, divided
Lemon juice, to taste
Salt and freshly ground pepper

In a jar with a hand blender or in a regular blender, combine the eggs, 1 teaspoon of the vinegar, and the mustard. Process to combine. With the motor running, very slowly add ½ cup of the oil. Blend until the oil is completely incorporated. Add the remaining 1 teaspoon vinegar. With the motor running, very slowly add the remaining oil in a steady stream. Blend in the lemon juice and salt and pepper and serve at once.

Yield: About 2 cups

EGGY SALAD DRESSING

There's no danger of illness from these eggs—they are hard-cooked! A great dressing for spinach and any green salad.

3 tablespoons white wine vinegar
2 tablespoons white wine
2 tablespoons Dijon-style mustard
1 small shallot, chopped
1 tablespoon minced onion
1 tablespoon fresh basil leaves or
   $3/4$ teaspoon dried
1 garlic clove
1 teaspoon sugar
Salt and freshly ground pepper, to taste
$2/3$ cup extra-virgin olive oil
1 hard-cooked egg, peeled and chopped

In a jar with a hand blender or in a food processor fitted with a steel blade, combine the vinegar, wine, mustard, shallot, onion, basil, garlic, and sugar. Blend until the garlic is finely chopped. Slowly add the oil, processing until the mixture is emulsified. Stir in the egg and salt and pepper to taste. Cover and chill the dressing until you are ready to use it. Let stand at room temperature for 5 minutes before mixing again and serving.

This will keep for up to 3 days in an airtight container in the refrigerator.

About $1^{1}/_{2}$ cups

REALLY RASPBERRY VINAIGRETTE

Raspberry vinaigrettes are extremely popular, and with good reason. The flavor is outstanding and works particularly well as a dressing for green salads that include tart and tangy lettuces and greens. It also makes a surprisingly good marinade for poultry. If you happen to have walnut oil on hand, use it here.

1 cup raspberries
1/2 cup white wine vinegar
2 tablespoons honey
1 tablespoon vegetable oil
Salt and freshly ground pepper
1 shallot, chopped

In a jar with a hand blender or in a food processor fitted with a steel blade, purée the raspberries. Strain, reserving the juice and discarding the seeds and pulp.

Return the raspberry juice to the jar or bowl and combine with the remaining ingredients. Use only 1 tablespoon honey. Blend to mix. Cover and chill the dressing until you are ready to use it. Let stand at room temperature for 5 minutes before mixing again and serving. Taste the dressing to make sure the sweet-sour balance is correct. If you want the vinaigrette to be sweeter, add the remaining 1 tablespoon honey.

This dressing will keep for up to 1 week in an airtight container in the refrigerator.

Yield: About 1 1/2 cups

BLUEBERRY VINAIGRETTE

Raspberries have already caught the attention of salad makers, but blueberries can also contribute their unique summery flavor in dressings and marinades.

1/3 **cup blueberries**
2 **tablespoons cider vinegar**
1 **tablespoon fresh lemon juice**
1 **tablespoon minced red onion**
1 **teaspoon sugar**
1/2 **teaspoon dry mustard**
1/4 **cup vegetable oil**
Salt and freshly ground pepper

In a jar with a hand blender or in a food processor fitted with a steel blade, combine the blueberries, vinegar, lemon juice, onion, sugar, and mustard. Blend until the blueberries are puréed. Strain, discarding the seeds and skin. Return the blueberry juice to the jar or bowl. With the motor running, slowly add the oil and continue processing until the oil is fully incorporated into the mixture. Add salt and pepper to taste. Cover and chill the dressing until you are ready to use it. Let stand at room temperature for 5 minutes before mixing again and serving.

This dressing will keep for up to 4 days in an airtight container in the refrigerator.

Variations: Huckleberries, blackberries, and raspberries can be used instead of the blueberries.

Yield: About 3/4 cup

Strawberry Surprise

The surprise is how wonderful fruity dressings go with green salads. It is also lovely on a grilled chicken breast bedded down on salad greens.

9 strawberries
1/3 cup vegetable oil
1/4 cup honey
2 tablespoons fresh grapefruit juice
2 tablespoons cider vinegar
1 teaspoon dry mustard
Freshly ground pepper

In a jar with a hand blender or in a food processor fitted with a steel blade, combine all the ingredients, adding pepper to taste. Blend until well mixed. Cover and chill the dressing until you are ready to use it. Let stand at room temperature for 5 minutes before mixing again and serving.

This dressing will keep for up to 2 days in an airtight container in the refrigerator.

Yield: About 1 cup

Papa's Papaya Dressing and Marinade

The only challenging part of this recipe is choosing a ripe papaya. Look for richly colored fruit that gives slightly to the touch. If it is still a little green, store it overnight in a paper bag. Refrigerate perfectly ripe fruit and use it quickly.

1 papaya, chopped
3 tablespoons chopped red onion
3 tablespoons white vinegar
1 tablespoon vegetable oil
1 tablespoon honey
1 tablespoon fresh sage leaves or
    1/4 teaspoon dried
Salt and freshly ground pepper

In a jar with a hand blender or in a food processor fitted with a steel blade, combine all the ingredients, adding salt and pepper to taste. Blend until well mixed. Cover and chill the dressing until you are ready to use it. Let stand at room temperature for 5 minutes before mixing again and serving.

This dressing will keep for up to 2 days in an airtight container in the refrigerator.

Yield: About 1 cup

My Mango Salad Dressing and Marinade

You'll taste the tropics in this lovely dressing. It makes an excellent marinade for poultry and seafood. If your mango lacks flavor, add 1 tablespoon honey to this dressing. Notice this contains no oil at all.

1 cup chopped mango
¼ cup fresh orange juice
3 tablespoons fresh lemon juice
3 tablespoons cider vinegar
1 teaspoon ground ginger
½ teaspoon grated orange zest
2 tablespoons chopped fresh cilantro
Salt and freshly ground pepper

In a jar with a hand blender or in a food processor fitted with a steel blade, combine all the ingredients except the cilantro, adding salt and pepper to taste. Blend until well mixed. Stir in the cilantro. Cover and chill the dressing until you are ready to use it. Let stand at room temperature for 5 minutes before mixing again and serving.

This dressing will keep for up to 2 days in an airtight container in the refrigerator.

Yield: About 1³/₄ cups

Pear Dressing

This dressing contains no oil, for those on a restrictive diet.

1/2 pear, diced
2 tablespoons fresh lemon juice
1 tablespoon honey
Salt and freshly ground pepper

In a jar with a hand blender or in a food processor fitted with a steel blade, combine all the ingredients, adding salt and pepper to taste. Blend until smooth. Cover and chill the dressing until you are ready to use it. Let stand at room temperature for 5 minutes before mixing again and serving. This is best served on the day it is made.

Yield: About 1/2 cup

Pear-Apple Surprise

This is wonderful as a dressing for finely shredded green cabbage or shredded romaine lettuce.

1 red apple, diced
1 pear, diced
1 small red onion, diced
3 tablespoons cider vinegar
1 tablespoon vegetable oil
1 tablespoon chopped fresh parsley

Combine all the ingredients in a medium-size bowl and stir well. Cover and refrigerate until you are ready to use it. This is best served on the day it is made.

Yield: About 1 1/4 cups

PEACH AND PEPPER DRESSING

This fruity mix is a treat served over grilled fish. As a dressing, it's fine over a mix of baby lettuce leaves. Note that it contains only 1 teaspoon of oil.

2 peaches, diced
1 to 2 jalapeños, diced
3 tablespoons finely chopped scallions
2 tablespoons finely chopped sweet red
    bell pepper
2 tablespoons finely chopped sweet green
    bell pepper
1 tablespoon fresh lime juice
1 tablespoon chopped fresh parsley
    (preferably Italian)
1 tablespoon chopped fresh cilantro
1 teaspoon extra-virgin olive oil
$1/2$ teaspoon ground cumin
Salt and freshly ground pepper

Combine all the ingredients in a medium-size bowl and stir well. Cover and refrigerate until you are ready to use it. This is best served on the day it is made.

Yield: About 1$1/2$ cups

LEMON RASPBERRY SALAD DRESSING

This dressing is wonderful dribbled over a wedge of iceberg lettuce. If you use low fat or non fat yogurt, the dressing will contain little or no oil.

1 cup lemon yogurt
1/2 tablespoons raspberry jelly
3 tablespoons fresh lemon juice
2 tablespoons finely chopped red onion
Salt and freshly ground pepper

Mix all the ingredients in a small bowl or jar and stir or shake to combine well.

Cover and refrigerate until you are ready to use it. This is best served on the day it is made.

This dressing will keep for up to 4 days in an airtight jar in the refrigerator.

Variations: Omit the onion, salt, and pepper and you have a lovely dressing for a fruit salad. Also, strawberry or apricot jelly may be substituted for the raspberry.

Yield: About 1 1/2 cups

GAZPACHO DRESSING

This is good over any salad greens. Notice it contains no oil at all.

1 tomato, chopped (see page 39)
1/2 cucumber, chopped
1 red bell pepper, chopped
1 small onion, chopped
1 garlic clove
1 tablespoon fresh lemon juice
1 tablespoon red wine vinegar
1 teaspoon Worcestershire sauce
Salt and freshly ground pepper

In a jar with a hand blender or in food processor fitted with a steel blade, combine the tomato, cucumber, bell pepper, onion, and garlic. Blend until well chopped. Stir in the lemon juice, vinegar, Worcestershire, and salt and pepper to taste. Cover and chill the dressing until you are ready to use it. Let stand at room temperature for 5 minutes before serving.

This dressing will keep for up to 2 days in an airtight container in the refrigerator.

Yield: About 2 cups

Roasted Pepper
Salad Dressing and Marinade

There is no oil in this dressing.

1 bell pepper, red, yellow, or green
2 tablespoons white wine vinegar
1 tablespoon fresh lemon juice
2 garlic cloves
1 tablespoon chopped fresh chives
Salt and pepper to taste

Over a gas flame or under a broiler, roast the bell pepper until charred and blistered all over, turning frequently. Place in a paper or plastic bag and set aside for 10 minutes to allow the bell pepper to steam. Then peel and chop it.

In a jar with a hand blender or in a food processor fitted with a steel blade, combine the bell pepper, vinegar, lemon juice, and garlic. Process until well chopped. Stir in the chives and salt and pepper to taste. Cover and chill the dressing until you are ready to use it. Let stand at room temperature for 5 minutes before serving.

This dressing will keep for up to 4 days in an airtight container in the refrigerator.

Yield: About 1/2 cup

MIGHTY MINT DRESSING

Notice there is no oil in this dressing.

1¹/₂ **cups fresh cilantro leaves**
¹/₄ **cup cider vinegar**
¹/₄ **cup honey**
2 tablespoons fresh mint leaves
1 tablespoon grated fresh ginger
1 jalapeño, seeded
Salt

In a jar with a hand blender or in a food processor fitted with a steel blade, combine all the ingredients, adding salt to taste. Blend until well chopped. Cover and chill the dressing until you are ready to use it. Let stand at room temperature for 5 minutes before serving.

This dressing will keep for up to 2 days in an airtight container in the refrigerator.

Yield: About 2 cups

FLYING R RANCH DRESSING

Ranch dressings are buttermilk dressings, usually flavored with onion and garlic and other seasonings. The original ranch dressing is said to have been created by the Henson Family, owners of Hidden Valley Ranch near Santa Barbara, California. They began selling their dressing as a dry mix shortly after World War II. This is my version.

1/3 cup buttermilk
1 tablespoon cider vinegar
1 tablespoon apple juice or cider
1 tablespoon fresh lemon juice
1 tablespoon sugar
1 garlic clove
1 scallion, white part only
1 tablespoon fresh thyme leaves or
   1/4 teaspoon dried
1 tablespoon fresh oregano leaves or
   1/4 teaspoon dried
1 egg yolk

1/3 cup vegetable oil
Salt and freshly ground pepper

In a jar with a hand blender or in a food processor fitted with a steel blade, combine the buttermilk, vinegar, apple juice, lemon juice, sugar, garlic, scallion, thyme, oregano, and egg yolk. Blend until the garlic, scallion, and herbs are finely chopped. With the motor running, slowly add the oil and continue processing until the oil is fully incorporated into the mixture. Add salt and pepper to taste. Cover and chill the dressing until you are ready to use it. Let stand at room temperature for 5 minutes before mixing again and serving.

This dressing is best served the day it is made.

Yield: About 1 1/4 cups

ROSY BUTTERMILK SALAD DRESSING

With the addition of ketchup, this buttermilk dressing tastes like a cross between a ranch dressing and a thousand island-type dressing.

3/4 cup mayonnaise
   (reduced-fat is acceptable)
1/3 cup plus 1 tablespoon buttermilk
1/3 cup plus 1 tablespoon ketchup
2 garlic cloves, minced
1 teaspoon Worcestershire sauce
1 teaspoon paprika
Salt and freshly ground pepper

Combine all the ingredients in a small bowl or jar, adding salt and pepper to taste. Stir or whisk well to combine. Cover and chill the dressing until you are ready to use it. Let stand at room temperature for 5 minutes before mixing again and serving.

This dressing will keep for up to 5 days in an airtight container in the refrigerator.

Yield: About 1 1/2 cups

CREAMY WINTER SPECIAL SALAD DRESSING

$^1/_2$ cup mayonnaise
  (reduced-fat is acceptable)
6 tablespoons buttermilk
2 tablespoons cider vinegar
1 shallot, minced
2 garlic cloves, minced
1 tablespoon fresh basil or
  $^3/_4$ teaspoon dried
1 tablespoon fresh thyme or
  $^3/_4$ teaspoon dried
Salt and freshly ground pepper

In a small bowl or jar, combine all the ingredients, adding salt and pepper to taste. Stir or shake to combine. Cover and chill the dressing until you are ready to use it. Let stand at room temperature for 5 minutes before mixing again and serving.

This dressing will keep for up to 5 days in an airtight container in the refrigerator.

Yield: About 1$^1/_4$ cups

Montana Herb Dressing

Horseradish and mustard give this ranch-style dressing a lot of zip. If you use nonfat buttermilk and yogurt, you will have a very healthy, low-fat dressing. It also makes a great dip for vegetables.

1/2 cup yogurt
1/2 cup mayonnaise
  (reduced-fat is acceptable)
1/4 cup buttermilk
1 tablespoon Dijon-style mustard
1 tablespoon prepared horseradish
1 tablespoon chopped fresh parsley
  (preferably Italian)
1 tablespoon fresh dill or
  1/2 teaspoon dried
Dash celery salt
Freshly ground pepper

In a small bowl or jar, combine all the ingredients, adding pepper to taste. Stir or shake to combine. Cover and chill the dressing until you are ready to use it. Let stand at room temperature for 5 minutes before mixing again and serving.

This dressing will keep for up to 5 days in an airtight container in the refrigerator.

Yield: About 1 1/2 cups

AIOLI

Aioli is nothing more than garlic-flavored mayonnaise. When made from scratch, it is simply heavenly. Even with the shortcut of using commercial mayonnaise, it makes a great dip for artichokes or seafood or a spread for sandwiches. Even a reduced-fat commercial mayonnaise is improved when made into Aioli.

1/2 cup mayonnaise (homemade, see page 69, or store-bought)
3 garlic cloves
Dash Tabasco sauce

In a jar with a hand blender or in a food processor fitted with a steel blade, combine the mayonnaise, garlic, and Tabasco. Process until the garlic is finely chopped. Cover and chill the dressing until you are ready to use it. If you are using a homemade mayonnaise, you should serve this on the day it is made. With commercial mayonnaise, this dressing will keep for up to 5 days in an airtight container in the refrigerator.

Variations: Add a squeeze of lemon or some chopped fresh herbs for extra flavor.

Yield: 1/2 cup

CAJUN MAYONNAISE

This makes a wonderful dressing for a seafood salad.

1 cup mayonnaise
   (reduced-fat is acceptable)
2 tablespoons fresh parsley leaves
   (preferably Italian)
1 tablespoon ketchup
2 teaspoons hot mustard
2 teaspoons prepared horseradish
2 teaspoons capers, rinsed and drained
1 teaspoon fresh tarragon or
   1/2 teaspoon dried
1 teaspoon fresh oregano or
   1/2 teaspoon dried
Dash Worcestershire sauce
Pinch cayenne
Salt

In a jar with a hand blender or in a food processor fitted with a steel blade, combine all the ingredients, adding salt to taste. Blend well. Cover and chill the dressing until you are ready to use it. Let stand at room temperature for 5 minutes before serving.

This dressing will keep for up to 2 weeks in an airtight container in the refrigerator.

Yield: 1 1/4 cups

RUSSIAN DRESSING

There's no finer spread for a roast beef or grilled Reuben sandwich than this homemade dressing.

1/3 **cup mayonnaise**
   (reduced-fat is acceptable)
2 **tablespoons finely chopped sweet**
   gherkins
1 **tablespoon finely chopped onion**
1 **tablespoon ketchup**
1/2 **teaspoon prepared horseradish**
Dash Worcestershire sauce
Freshly ground pepper

Combine all the ingredients in a small bowl or jar, adding pepper to taste. Stir well to combine. Cover and chill the dressing until you are ready to use it. Let stand at room temperature for 5 minutes before serving.

This dressing will keep for up to 2 weeks in an airtight container in the refrigerator.

Yield: About 1/2 cup

THOUSAND ISLAND DRESSING

$^1/_3$ cup mayonnaise
   (reduced-fat is acceptable)
$^1/_3$ cup sour cream
$^1/_4$ cup fresh lemon juice
$^1/_4$ cup chili sauce or ketchup
$^1/_4$ cup finely chopped green bell pepper
2 tablespoons finely chopped onion
1 tablespoon vegetable oil
1 tablespoon chopped fresh parsley
   (preferably Italian)
Pinch cayenne

Combine all the ingredients in a small bowl or jar. Stir well to combine. Cover and chill the dressing until you are ready to use it. Let stand at room temperature for 5 minutes before serving.

This dressing will keep for up to 2 weeks in an airtight container in the refrigerator.

Yield: $1^2/_3$ cups

LOW-CAL THOUSAND ISLAND DRESSING

If you are trying to avoid fat, consider this version of Thousand Island Dressing.

¹/₂ cup cottage cheese
5 tablespoons tomato juice
3 tablespoons milk
1¹/₂ teaspoons sugar
2 tablespoons finely chopped onion
2 tablespoons finely chopped green bell pepper
1 tablespoon finely chopped dill pickle
Salt and freshly ground pepper

In a jar with a hand blender or in a food processor fitted with a steel blade, combine the cottage cheese, tomato juice, milk, and sugar. Blend until smooth. Stir in the onion, green pepper, pickle, and salt and pepper to taste. Cover and chill the dressing until you are ready to use it. Let stand at room temperature for 5 minutes before serving.

This dressing will keep for up to 4 days in an airtight container in the refrigerator.

Yield: About ¹/₄ cup

SPANISH OLIVE DRESSING

This is a delicious choice for a seafood salad. I like to combine crab, artichoke hearts, and tomatoes and serve the mixture on a bed of lettuce, topped with this dressing.

1/2 cup mayonnaise
    (reduced-fat is acceptable)
2 tablespoons milk
2 tablespoons finely chopped stuffed
    Spanish olives
1 tablespoon finely chopped green
    bell pepper
1 tablespoon finely chopped onion
1 tablespoon chili sauce
Freshly ground pepper

Combine all the ingredients in a small bowl or jar, adding pepper to taste. Stir well to combine. Cover and chill the dressing until you are ready to use it. Let stand at room temperature for 5 minutes before serving.

This dressing will keep for up to 2 weeks in an airtight container in the refrigerator.

Yield: About 1 cup

TANGY GARLIC SALAD DRESSING

10 tablespoons mayonnaise
   (reduced-fat is acceptable)
3 tablespoons cider vinegar
3 tablespoons fresh parsley leaves
   (preferably Italian)
2 tablespoons Dijon-style mustard
2 tablespoons ketchup
2 garlic cloves
Pinch cayenne
Salt and freshly ground pepper

In a jar with a hand blender or in a food processor fitted with a steel blade, combine all the ingredients, adding salt and pepper to taste. Blend well. Cover and chill the dressing until you are ready to use it. Let stand at room temperature for 5 minutes before serving.

This dressing will keep for up to 2 weeks in an airtight container in the refrigerator.

Yield: About 1¹/₄ cups

LOUIS DRESSING

This dressing is based on an old American classic: Crab Louis, which was made with crabmeat and a mayonnaise-based dressing. The dish is claimed by at least two different San Francisco hotel dining rooms, as well as by the chef at the Olympic Club in Seattle, Washington. The recipe harks back to the days when no one worried about calories, and the result was some very delicious eating.

1 cup mayonnaise
   (reduced-fat is acceptable)
1/4 cup chili sauce
2 scallions, thinly sliced
1 teaspoon fresh lemon juice
Salt and freshly ground pepper
1/4 cup whipping cream

In a medium-size bowl, combine the mayonnaise, chili sauce, scallions, lemon juice, and salt and pepper to taste. Whisk together well.

In a separate jar or bowl, whip the cream with a hand blender or mixer until soft peaks form. Whisk the cream into the mayonnaise mixture gently but thoroughly. Cover and chill the dressing until you are ready to use it. Let stand at room temperature for 5 minutes before serving. This dressing is at its best on the day it is made.

Yield: About 1 1/2 cups

ROASTED GARLIC SALAD DRESSING

1 whole garlic bulb
1 teaspoon extra-virgin olive oil
3 tablespoons sour cream
2 tablespoons mayonnaise
     (reduced-fat is acceptable)
2 tablespoons yogurt
2 scallions, chopped
1½ tablespoons cider vinegar
Salt and freshly ground pepper

Preheat the oven to 375° F. Cut off the point top of the garlic bulb, removing about 1/2 inch. Place cut side down on a piece of aluminum foil and drizzle with oil. Wrap up in the foil and bake for 40 minutes. Let cool. Squeeze the garlic from the cloves.

In a jar with a hand blender or in a food processor fitted with a steel blade, combine the garlic purée with the remaining ingredients. Blend until smooth. Cover and chill the dressing until you are ready to use it. Let stand at room temperature for 5 minutes before serving.

This dressing will keep for up to 4 days in an airtight container in the refrigerator.

Yield: About ¾ cup

Green Goddess Dressing

Another American classic, this salad dressing is made with mayonnaise, anchovies, and tarragon. The dressing was created in the 1920s at Palace Hotel in San Francisco at the request of an actor who was appearing in town in a play entitled "The Green Goddess." The play was later made into a film, but the dressing is more famous.

1 1/2 cups mayonnaise
(reduced-fat is acceptable)
1/2 cup fresh parsley leaves
(preferably Italian)
1 small onion, chopped
2 tablespoons cider vinegar
2 tablespoons fresh tarragon or 1 teaspoon
dried
1 1/2 tablespoons anchovy paste
3 tablespoons thinly sliced fresh chives

In a jar with a hand blender or in a food processor fitted with a steel blade, combine the mayonnaise, parsley, onion, vinegar, tarragon, and anchovy paste. Process until smooth. Stir in the chives. Cover and chill the dressing until you are ready to use it. Let stand at room temperature for 5 minutes before serving.

This dressing will keep for up to 5 days in an airtight container in the refrigerator.

Yield: About 2 1/2 cups

CREAMY PEPPER-PARMESAN SALAD DRESSING

*This creamy cheese dressing is flavored with lots
of pepper. I usually make it with freshly grated
Parmesan, but Romano makes a good substitute,
and is a nice change of pace.*

¼ cup mayonnaise
    (reduced-fat is acceptable)
¼ cup milk
2 tablespoons freshly grated
    Parmesan cheese
2 tablespoons fresh lemon juice
1 tablespoon cider vinegar
1 tablespoon water
2 teaspoons minced onion
1 teaspoon freshly ground pepper
Dash Tabasco sauce
Dash Worcestershire sauce
Salt

Combine all the ingredients in a bowl or jar,
adding salt to taste. Stir or shake well to combine. Cover and chill the dressing until you are
ready to use it. Let stand at room temperature
for 5 minutes before serving.

This dressing will keep for up to 4 days in
an airtight container in the refrigerator.

Yield: About 1 cup

CREAMY DIJON SALAD DRESSING

The balance of flavors in this dressing is quite good.

1/2 cup mayonnaise
   (reduced-fat is acceptable)
2 tablespoons red wine vinegar
1 garlic clove, finely chopped
2 teaspoons Dijon-style mustard
2 teaspoons Worcestershire sauce
1 teaspoon anchovy paste
Freshly ground pepper

Combine all the ingredients in a bowl or jar, adding salt to taste. Stir or shake well to combine. Cover and chill the dressing until you are ready to use it. Let stand at room temperature for 5 minutes before serving.

This dressing will keep for up to 2 weeks in an airtight container in the refrigerator.

Yield: About 3/4 cup

HOLIDAY SPECIAL SALAD DRESSING

The horseradish in this dressing makes this dressing very unusual.

¹/₄ cup mayonnaise
   (reduced-fat is acceptable)
¹/₂ cup yogurt
2 tablespoons sour cream
2 teaspoons prepared horseradish
1 teaspoon Dijon-style mustard
2 garlic cloves
2 teaspoons thinly sliced fresh chives
Salt and freshly ground pepper

In a jar with a hand blender or in a food processor fitted with a steel blade, combine the mayonnaise, yogurt, sour cream, horseradish, mustard, and garlic. Process until smooth. Stir in the chives. Add salt and pepper to taste. Cover and chill the dressing until you are ready to use it. Let stand at room temperature for 5 minutes before serving.

This dressing will keep for up to 5 days in an airtight container in the refrigerator.

Yield: About ³/₄ cup

CUCUMBER DRESSING

If you make this with mayonnaise (reduced-fat is acceptable), you have a very low-fat dressing. The cucumber gives this dressing body and a very light flavor.

3/4 cup mayonnaise
(reduced-fat is acceptable)
1 tablespoon fresh lemon juice
1 tablespoon cider vinegar
1 cucumber, chopped
1 celery stalk, diced
4 stuffed green olives, minced
Pinch chili powder
Salt and freshly ground pepper

In a jar with a hand blender or in a food processor fitted with a steel blade, combine all the ingredients, adding salt and pepper to taste. Process until smooth. Cover and chill the dressing until you are ready to use it. Let stand at room temperature for 5 minutes before serving.

This dressing will keep for up to 5 days in an airtight container in the refrigerator.

Yield: About 1¹/₂ cups

FLATLANDER'S FAVORITE

This dressing is very thick, with hard-boiled eggs giving the dressing its flavor and texture. It makes a very good dressing for asparagus. The combination of eggs and asparagus resonates with spring.

3 hard-cooked eggs, divided
3 tablespoons white wine vinegar
2 tablespoons Dijon-style mustard
6 tablespoons extra-virgin olive oil
¹/₃ cup yogurt
3 scallions, minced
Salt and freshly ground pepper

In a medium-size bowl, combine 2 of the egg yolks with the vinegar and mustard and mash to a paste. Slowly add the oil, while whisking constantly. Continue whisking until the dressing is emulsified. Chop the remaining egg whites and 1 egg yolk and stir into the dressing along with the yogurt, scallions, and salt and pepper to taste. Cover and chill the dressing until you are ready to use it. Let stand at room temperature for 5 minutes before serving.

This dressing will keep for up to 2 days in an airtight container in the refrigerator.

Yield: 1¹/₂ cups

CURRY SALAD DRESSING

Curry powder and mango chutney give this creamy dressing its distinctively exotic flavor. It is a great dressing to use with a fruit salad and is delicious on a spinach-and-mandarin orange salad.

1/4 cup whipping cream
1 1/2 tablespoons white wine vinegar
1 1/2 tablespoons mango chutney
1 teaspoon vegetable oil
1 teaspoon grated ginger
1/2 teaspoon curry powder
Pinch cayenne
Salt and freshly ground pepper

In a jar with a hand blender or in a food processor fitted with a steel blade, combine all the ingredients, adding salt and pepper to taste. Process until smooth. Cover and chill the dressing until you are ready to use it. Let stand at room temperature for 5 minutes before serving.

This dressing will keep for up to 2 days in an airtight container in the refrigerator.

Yield: About 1/2 cup

Texas Special Salad Dressing

1/2 cup yogurt
1 tablespoon vegetable oil
2 teaspoons fresh lemon juice
2 teaspoons Dijon-style mustard
2 teaspoons chopped fresh parsley
1 teaspoon sugar
Pinch cayenne
Salt and freshly ground pepper
1 hard-cooked egg

In a small bowl, mix together all the ingredients except the egg, adding salt and pepper to taste. Stir well. If desired, chop the egg and add to the dressing. Or reserve the egg for use as a garnish, chopping it just before serving. Cover and chill the dressing until you are ready to use it. Let stand at room temperature for 5 minutes before serving.

Without the egg, this dressing will keep for up to 5 days in an airtight container in the refrigerator; with the egg, store it for up to 2 days.

Yield: About 3/4 cup

CREAMIEST PARMESAN DRESSING

Although blue cheese comes to mind when we think of cheese dressings, Parmesan lends great flavor to a dressing. This creamy Parmesan dressing makes a delicious dip for vegetables.

$1/4$ cup mayonnaise (reduced-fat is
   acceptable)
$1/4$ cup freshly grated Parmesan cheese
3 tablespoons white wine vinegar
2 tablespoons sour cream
2 tablespoons chopped fresh parsley
1 tablespoon Dijon-style mustard
Pinch fine herbes
Salt and freshly ground pepper
$1/3$ cup vegetable oil

In a small bowl, mix together all the ingredients except the oil, adding salt and pepper to taste. Whisk well. Slowly add the oil, whisking constantly, until the dressing is emulsified. Cover and chill the dressing until you are ready to use it. Let stand at room temperature for 5 minutes before serving.

This dressing will keep for up to 5 days in an airtight container in the refrigerator.

Yield: About 1$1/2$ cups

Great Gorgonzola Salad Dressing

Blue cheese is crumbly, so it is easy to break it into small crumbs for adding to a dressing. But if you prefer even-size bits in the dressing, try this trick: Place the cheese in the freezer for 10 minutes. Then grate the cheese with a box grater. You'll be pleased with the results!

3/4 cup mayonnaise
    (reduced-fat is acceptable)
3 tablespoons cider vinegar
1 1/2 tablespoons ketchup
1 garlic clove
1 teaspoon Worcestershire sauce
Freshly ground pepper
1/2 cup crumbled or grated Gorgonzola
    cheese

In a jar with a hand blender or in a food processor fitted with a steel blade, combine all the ingredients, except the cheese, adding pepper to taste. Process until smooth. Stir in the cheese. Cover and chill the dressing until you are ready to use it. Let stand at room temperature for 5 minutes before serving.

This dressing will keep for up to 4 days in an airtight container in the refrigerator.

Yield: About 1 1/2 cups

BOB'S BLUE CHEESE DRESSING

$^{1}/_{2}$ cup mayonnaise
   (reduced-fat is acceptable)
5 tablespoons milk
Juice of $^{1}/_{2}$ lemon
1 tablespoon minced onion
1 garlic clove, minced
$^{1}/_{2}$ teaspoon Worcestershire sauce
Salt and freshly ground pepper
$^{1}/_{2}$ cup crumbled blue cheese

In a bowl or jar, combine all the ingredients except the cheese, adding salt and pepper to taste. Stir or shake to mix well. Add the cheese and stir lightly. Cover and chill the dressing until you are ready to use it. Let stand at room temperature for 5 minutes before serving.

This dressing will keep for up to 4 days in an airtight container in the refrigerator.

Yield: About 1$^{1}/_{4}$ cups

BLUE CHEESE DRESSING 2

1 cup crumbled blue cheese
³/₄ cup sour cream
¹/₄ cup mayonnaise (reduced-fat is
    acceptable)
2 garlic cloves, minced
1 tablespoon red wine vinegar
Salt and freshly ground pepper

In a jar with a hand blender or in a food processor fitted with a steel blade, combine all the ingredients, adding salt and pepper to taste. Process briefly. Cover and chill the dressing until you are ready to use it. Let stand at room temperature for 5 minutes before serving.

This dressing will keep for up to 4 days in an airtight container in the refrigerator.

Yield: About 2 cups

GOAT CHEESE DRESSING

²/₃ cup crumbled soft goat cheese (chèvre)
5 tablespoons sour cream
2 tablespoons vegetable oil
1¹/₂ tablespoons cider vinegar
1 tablespoon fresh lemon juice
3 scallions, thinly sliced
¹/₂ teaspoon cayenne
Salt and freshly ground pepper

In a bowl or jar, combine all the ingredients except the cheese, adding salt and pepper to taste. Stir to mix well. Cover and chill the dressing until you are ready to use it. Let stand at room temperature for 5 minutes before serving.

This dressing will keep for up to 4 days in an airtight container in the refrigerator.

Yield: About 1¹/₄ cups

CREAMY TOFU SALAD DRESSING

1/2 **pound firm tofu**
2 **tablespoons extra-virgin olive oil**
2 **tablespoons fresh lemon juice**
1 **tablespoon soy sauce**
2 **garlic cloves, minced**
1 **teaspoon fresh dill or** 1/4 **teaspoon dried**
1/2 **teaspoon chili powder**
Freshly ground pepper

In a jar with a hand blender or in a food processor fitted with a steel blade, combine all the ingredients, adding pepper to taste. Process until smooth. Cover and chill the dressing until you are ready to use it. Let stand at room temperature for 5 minutes before serving.

This dressing will keep for up to 4 days in an airtight container in the refrigerator.

Yield: About 1 1/4 cups

Sesame Tofu Salad Dressing

1/4 **pound tofu, drained**
1/3 **cup plus 1 tablespoon yogurt**
2 **tablespoons fresh lemon juice**
1 **tablespoon tahini**
1 **tablespoon toasted sesame oil**
2 **scallions, sliced**
2 **teaspoons grated ginger**
1 **teaspoon honey**
Freshly ground pepper

In a jar with a hand blender or in a food processor fitted with a steel blade, combine all the ingredients, adding pepper to taste. Process until smooth. Cover and chill the dressing until you are ready to use it. Let stand at room temperature for 5 minutes before serving.

This dressing will keep for up to 4 days in an airtight container in the refrigerator.

Yield: About 11/4 **cups**

Specialty Cookbooks from The Crossing Press

Biscotti, Brownies, and Bars

By Terri Henry

This collection of easy-to-follow recipes presents more than 70 recipes for cookies baked in a pan. Terri Henry is a food stylist and caterer.

$6.95 • Paper • ISBN 0-89594-901-6

Old World Breads

By Charel Scheele

In this authentic collection, the art of old world bread-making is available to everyone. Instructions are given to get brick oven results from an ordinary oven using a simple clay flower-pot saucer.

$6.95 • Paper • ISBN 0-89594-902-4

Pestos! Cooking with Herb Pastes

By Dorothy Rankin

"An inventive and tasteful collection—it makes the possibilities of herb pastes enticing."
—*Publishers Weekly*

$8.95 • Paper • ISBN 0-89594-180-5

Salsas!

By Andrea Chesman

"Appeals to me because of the recipes' originality and far-ranging usefulness."
—Elliot Mackle, *Creative Loafing*

$8.95 • Paper • ISBN 0-89594-178-3

Sauces for Pasta!

By K. Trabant with A. Chesman

"This little book has my favorite new and old sauces."
—Grace Kirschenbaum, *World of Cookbooks*

$8.95 • Paper • ISBN 0-89594-403-0

Sun-Dried Tomatoes

By Andrea Chesman

Chesman's simple recipes include a savory selection of appetizers, salads, pastas, and breads as well as instructions for drying tomatoes at home.

$6.95 • Paper • ISBN 0-89594-900-8

To receive a current catalog from The Crossing Press, please call toll-free, 800-777-1048.
Visit our Website on the Internet at: www.crossingpress.com

Cookbooks from The Crossing Press

Fiery Appetizers:
70 Spicy Hot Hors d'Oeuvres
By Dave DeWitt and Nancy Gerlach

This sizzling collection offers easy-to-follow recipes for seventy spicy-got appetizers guaranteed to satisfy the most discerning of heat-seeking palates.

$8.95 • Paper • ISBN 0-89594-785-4

Great Salsas by the Boss of Sauce
From the Southwest & Points Beyond
By W. C. Longacre and Dave DeWitt

Longacre brings a creative collection of recipes from the southwest, Mexico, Asia, and the Caribbean into your kitchen.

$12.95 • Paper • ISBN 0-89594-817-6

The Great Barbecue Companion
By Bruce Bjorkman

A collection of sauces covering the best barbecue flavors: sweet, savory, hot, and spicy — sometimes mixing all four. "A mouth-watering array of recipes…add this one to your library."

—National Barbecue News

$12.95 • Paper • ISBN 0-89594-806-0

Jerk: Barbecue from Jamaica
By Helen Willinsky

"An inspired collection of fiery recipes from the Caribbean islands written by an expert on the topic." *—Gourmet Retailer*

$12.95 • Paper • ISBN 0-89594-439-1

Marinades: Dry Rubs, Pastes & Marinades for Poultry, Meat, Seafood, Cheese & Vegetables
By Jim Tarantino

Tarantino recreates marinades and flavoring pastes from all over the world, and provides instructions for preparing seafood, poultry, meat, vegetables, and cheese—indoors and out.

$16.95 • Paper • ISBN 0-89594-531-2

The Hot Sauce Bible
By Dave DeWitt and Chuck Evans

The Hot Sauce Bible takes you on a journey exploring the role of hot sauces and chile peppers from around the world, with recipes, facts, folklore, anecdotes, web sites and a comprehensive cataloging of 1,600 hot sauces.

$20.00 • Paper • ISBN 0-89594-760-9